GLARING

Glaring
© 2020 Benjamin Krusling

All rights reserved. No part of this book may be used or reproduced without prior permission of the publisher.

Passage Series #1
First Edition, 2020
Edition of 1,000 copies
ISBN: 978-1-7359242-0-5
Library of Congress Control Number: 202094

Cover concept, photography, and design by Europium (Julia Andréone and Ghazaal Vojdani)
Copy edited by Rachel Valinsky and Corinne Butta
Typesetting by Simran Ankolkar
Typeset in Gerstner Programm and Nimbus Roman No. 9
Printed at KOPA, Lithuania

Distributed by Small Press Distribution (SPD)
www.spdbooks.org

Published by Wendy's Subway
379 Bushwick Avenue
Brooklyn, NY 11206
wendyssubway.com

Wendy's Subway is a non-profit reading room, writing space, and independent publisher located in Brooklyn.

Glaring was selected for the 2019 Wendy's Subway Open Reading Period judged by Lucy Ives.

The Passage Series publishes titles by emerging writers and artists whose work manifests in innovative, hybrid, and cross-genre forms that imagine new possibilities and expressions of the poetic, the political, and the social.

The Passage Series is supported, in part, by public funds from the New York City Department of Cultural Affairs in Partnership with the City Council. *Glaring* is also supported, in part, by a regrant awarded and administered by the Community of Literary Magazines and Presses (CLMP). CLMP's NYS regrant programs are made possible by the New York State Council on the Arts with the support of Governor Andrew M. Cuomo and the New York State Legislature.

GLARING

Benjamin Krusling

WENDY'S SUBWAY

For LB & G

anyone who does not agree is cut off by the newsmen, not allowed to speak. They merely reflect our policy. The trial jury will have to not have heard of the invasion not to have seen the news being on it will depend on their ignorance.

so the unfolding of phenomena is dependent on ignorance, and we would stop it have it come back in if we were not that.

—Leslie Scalapino, from "What/Person?"

the peace of the board, we might say, is subtended by the knocking of the poltergeist.

—Hortense Spillers, "Peter's Pans: Eating in the Diaspora"

CONTENTS

the artifact being thought the most beautiful thing	11
listen up	15
IN THE LIGHTS , I'M DAZZLED , EASILY	19
E C S T A T I C S	63
GRAPES	81
IN POPEYES (*the chamber won't produce resonant volume , then love of the other moves them to silence*	111
pleasure is stubborn / in retrospect	129
Acknowledgments	133

the artifact being thought
the most beautiful thing

I thought I was near where Malcolm was shot , then I realized I was wrong . we were blessed with these sensitivities , navigating a landscape that varies its networks of trouble ,

change over time .

in fact , the building , which was not where I was – though I was near there – is decorated with *terra-cotta glazed polychromy , encrustations and cornices* , gaudy colors in the Hellenistic style .

my face crushed against the wiki page on which I was reading this , collecting material for a treatment .

I was there , having realized I was wrong and the memory of being somewhere else . was I being spoken to I wondered , not being the only voice possible in that area .

the idea of violence from an old photograph , the setting of someone up , is digital . weaving these things through one another as habit and then intent . because I was scared?

and without equipment . navigating that , gaudily .

then that historical feeling , thinking one is where something happened that one is thinking about . then not being there , but feeling that .

the world *peopled* as it is with *hallucinations* , justice being not among them , but thought of also . experiencing conspiracy as a digital product .

anxious , setting the scene while isolating the voice , people themselves being so small on the sidewalk .

people themselves dying so violently , the memory of that hanging . as at that moment , I was having my small , different experience , heading more slowly and apparently elsewhere .

being young after all , looking upwards , as I'm describing myself at that time . encrustations looming .

listen up

excess is advancing , this inhibition could go again , my obligations shake
        off the leg like a tumble of lint . I'm a stable
    cultural accident , brain blockchained to the
police
        station as I walk to the co-op and back , a unit
      of shook economy , a culture , tended ,
for the driftless Midwestern thought
        tank . break . black moonlight break
            black window .
we owe each other a yes . we will win , for we have no other option .
        we want the energy of high design to lift
      debris from our hearts , to call our fathers on the
   phone , make them stop
           this barbarous oiling . but there's only us
        here , not consolation . etc . I'm iridescent
in the university office , handing intellectual property to the
    moderate secretary , salaried ,
           so supportive , then a word from my heart
           sweeps oxygen into me ,
                then a worm in my heart , then ,
                trust , attention ?
   in the club one night the song I heard was only broken glass
      then I knew it , I was sick , I said I'm sick , I'm up , I am

IN THE LIGHTS , I'M DAZZLED , EASILY

to heaven , on a mule

Spurious !
      (Helene Johnson

      my dream of heaven was an ice cream factory , but it echoed blackface heaven from a few minutes earlier . & all wishes ,

      brained on the marvel of televised limbo where production assistants line up lights and vanish , drag social pain into procedures

      that taste great on camera . (people ! in that sense , reviewing memory produces artifacts , long static renditions

      of blackface (? heaven ? so they try to shred the Bush years with vocal runs . it's a room with floor to ceiling mirrors & people spread their arms there

      to sing to place the face at the center to tell the world childhood is sweet though it tastes like power over , though it tastes like pistachio . these are eyes I make the world so careful with . long static . long talk . well , you say you want a strong feeling .

have one . or someone will think you're withholding . (in your tight t-shirt . tight tight tight . in your canada goose and gloves .

it's like fed logic . *depression-fighting escapism* . childhood is so sweet , they say , as they go house to house killing on a thick recursive loop .

& their faces drip , they're wet with effort .

let's get it !

I was depressed when I said anything before
                                 now I'm good ! feeling better

down with pigs, ICE, the *New York Times*
                                 throw it out ! close the prisons

shout out C.L.R. James once , twice
                                 I love 808s ! bass , drones

my cousin Kiah ! Sophia !
                                 look at us breaking cycles

can't forget An and my good friends
                                 I love artists ! first thought best

even if I never write another line, I'll find a decent way to live
                   if I have to breathe the most outrageous trouble

if I have to let everyone else slide
                   pull the oxygen masks over their beautiful baby faces !

I might have to die !

        what most people do is not at all easy !

I take medication and drink

        then it only takes a glass to really wipe me out

this time I'm more attentive to my whole feeling apparatus !

my mom tells me not to mix liquor and pills

        as I watch her very high-risk behavior !

I love you mom ! be safe !   I love you moon ! be full

        drugs kill !

for so long I had this little marriage fantasy

        having never seen it close or work

I was really a low life !

        now I'm back and twice as necessary !

the buildings today were hot they cracked with anger !

        we were on the same page !

I feel very sure I'm good

                I know that I'm feeling

tomorrow will be here like a firebomb !

friendship is roughly everywhere , thanks

the uniformed person puts traffic cones
    down in neat rows , they're bright

        orange . weeping . what's next

    is I'm happy for your jazz concern . it's all sexual

& if I pushed it clear we'd still be on the street
    right inside the boundary . I'm so happy . there's nothing
    going on .

Saretta was right about *winning* – full of information , none glowing ,
    synthetic color in the limbic motor .

it's just people look so good
    when you trust them
        & you don't look

millenarian amoxicillic blues

        very missing caramel : very ugly sundae , hostile *can I help you* from a man in a suit at a building downtown . but , we're under a similar heel .

        I'm a vandal , the grid is on ice with my common plantings . no machine can make me whole .

        in the DC summer , I was devastated , that fire brought lines to my face (BD . and workers
    in these liberal fits and patterns
on the same page of quote pragmatism . I'm a black American taxpayer
        but when I woke from my dream
of jogger shopping , I was still in this world of enclosure , with
        the coast in me , the climax . then I think : the police are strong with this one . it's drama . everything's getting cloned .

        and in the New York summer , I was devastated .
        and in the Cincinnati summer
I was devastated . and in the Iowa summer

        — but not to fix it ? the zoo paid my grandma a lot to leave her home . that old blue house
    was barely even blue as it fell off the side of the road .
        when you think of peace , you're sick , my friend .

                your face is lit
with the revolution's problems .
                        as for me , who loves to not suffer , I'm bathed in
                        the brilliant lights
of attention where racist painters craft a stupid response:
                        the circus is returning , with bells and bombs on ,
calling on us all to carry that cold to the subway and home .

issa sonnet

it's a point of fact   harm is dramatically under
nourished .   my white father's mad again
and I'm on a journey to the supermarket ,
the classroom where floors are stained with indigo ,
where dissociative tax bracketers
have visions of burning police vehicles .
(what's that look like in my eyes ? did you think
of black wizardry ? are you dripping with sauce ?
dreaming seems great cuz there's always examples
loaded in the pornographic myth-maker . the truth is that
the strangling is known in certain places
as singing . the truth is you agree . violence is cool .
that's why you'd sell your soul for family .
that's why I'm here with fear and tears about it .

another one

it's always on sight cuz pleasure is nowhere ,

why white lights passing don't give themselves

to formal imagination . there's a bomb

in that iPhone , so what ? one walks in the schoolhouse

, gets sat down all over , blood , gets psychosocially thinned

by thirsty adults . they're yelling obscenities

at social optimism . and it's all so cruel , the sky is carved

into gold bars by bitcoin hoarders ...

so I'm made to feel shame for being shamed

for being poor now too ? everyone has tendencies

but even planets get rearranged , with great variance –

jubilance , blood ! I know . I'm grown

cuz my mind makes pills that my heart

swallows dutifully , cuz the paranoid position

is the best guest I have . I'd just felt I'd been so evil

being young , having no idea what people were doing .

they were pointing at miserable difference

saying look who sleeps rougher than me ! and teething

well , there *is* no greater love

o , ecstatic plenitude in my good head
I wake up to the churning of my heart's shallow water ,

lustful and prostrate beneath the tortured lights
of unity . we're non-stop distinct

as we touch adulthood's dripping wrist ,
its neon wet neck , as we negotiate

the coupling that has us draped
from wire hangers .

real love is such syntactic change ,
twisted in the melodramatic glare

of our grabbing despair by the foot ,
dry-heaving towards the pornographic .

under the face's blue weight , you think
the heart is good without these gifts .

you think how in the brain's red birth
the chest comes forward , the eyes click ,

the two parties are established ,
then the lips begin their scrambled flashing .

words seen in the sense of portals / the
night makes compassion happen / in the sense
of one narrow read of *ethnic* embitterment /
wherein the amnesiac field is bled by visual data
/ where twenty chains dance in the mirror (don
q) / in the sense of the voice as it were hopping
the discontinuous turnstile / – as everyone
knows I'm in love / the mind is *filled* / so one
sees space occur visually between two people
/ space when there's none there is there ? / in
the night where black makes matter happen
/ where het love is a freaky war machine / &
one's psychosexual nightmare makes phantoms
that stack sandpaper in the linen closet / as if
the words could be seen doing that / there's no
one here but you / *pure present and always tense*
(Hortense Spillers) / it's night

no stars no stars no stars no stars no stars no stars nostsars nosatrs

nosatrs nosatrs nosatrs nostras noastras nosatars nostars no stars

nostars nos tars no stars no stars no stars no starts no stars no stars

no stars nostats no stars no stars no stars no stars no stars no tstrs

no stars nosatrs no satrs no satrs no satrs nostrad nosatrds nostars

no stars no stars no stars no stars no stars no stars no stars nostars

no stars no stars nostars nos tars no stars no stars no stras nostars

nostars n stars nostars no stars no atrs no stars nostars no stars ostars no stars no stars nostars no satrs nosars nostrars nost arsr no stars nosars no stars no stars o srars no starts no stars no stars no stars no stars no stars no stars no stars no stars nostars ostars nostars no stsra no stars no stars n ostars no tstars nonosarrs no tstars no stars no starts onsta nostars nosatrs nostars nostars nostars notasrs nostars npstars nostars nostars no starts nostarts nostars no sirens siresns nisresn sirens nisrens sirens nsirens sirens isrens isrens siresns siresns sirens ssirens sirens sirens sirens isresns sirens sirens sirens sirens sirens sirens sirens sirens sirens sirens isrens sirens sirens sirens sirens sirens sirens sirens sirens sirens sirens no sirens isrens soresn sreisn sorejsn no sirens nosreisn nosriens nosriens soreins soriens soreins no sriens no sirens no sirens no sirens no sirens no sirens no sirens no sirens no sirens no sreins ons riens no sirens no sirens nno sirens no sirens no sirens no sirens no sirens no sirens no sirens no siensn osn reisn snoiene sno riens no sirens no sirens no sirens no sirens no sirens no sirens no clothe sno cloths no clothes no clothes no clothes no clothes no clothes no clothes no clothes no clothes no clothes no clothes no clotehs no clothes no clothes no clothes no clothes no clothes no clothes no clithes no clothes no clothes no clothes noc tloehs no clothes no clothes no clothes no clothers no cotles no coltes no clthes no clothes not lcothes no clothes no lcothes no lcohtes no closthets no clostehts no cloethes no clothes n lcohd no closehts no slothes no clothes sno clothes no slothes no clothes no clothes no clothes no family no family no family no fiamil no family no family no family no family no family no family no family no family no family no family no family no family foaml no family no family no family nofami no family no family no family no famyli fno famyli fnoy family no framliy no framoly no family no family no family no ammgo no mabmly no family no family no family ofamily no family no family nos night night night night night night night night night nighti night night nighti night night night night no night night no night no night no night no night no night no night no night no night no nightno night no nightn no hight no night no ngith no ngiht noight no ight no night no night no night no night no night no night no nigut no night no night no night no night no night no night no night no night no night no night no nightn ihgt nno night no night no night no night no ight no night no night no night no night no night no night no night no night no night no

I will live with intent not glaring & ripping

today I did the opposite of what I say I should

the whole top half of me just leaned down

sorry I'm rehearsing on the side of the road thinking about feeling right

look I'm running ! and not unhappy to
                              flowers flowing hotly from my eyes

all these ships passing cuz it's all this fog around

all this loud myth for how to get it cracking for the undercommons

it's the club scene you think

I don't know why I don't just send all my desire forward

look I can't be holding my own hand through the world feet falling asleep

I want a hug   the work I do is full of pain

I have to know how things will brush my heart

let the people I love palm me in the temple

to trust !   and I will

(the referee lifts my fist up

lethologica

poverty(yyy) made me   roll my eyes open, whites showing,
forget the names of trees and creatures (brain damage) —
what you call it when even the face of god
is matte & filtered   out to where I am

on fire (   ) the truth , that even the fruits of our eyes spoil
I'm inside , upset by my impressions

is that sense ? our sun ascends
        in obscene silence

the soles of my sister turn to stone (   ) and I go
rampaging over the earth,
        giving off black product , black as exhaust is

your choice ! work or leave
        I see   so   isolation
        the syllables split   roll open

the situation starts assuming (
) speechless romantic positions

seasons go by like I'm binge watching

youth passes, but there's no opposite

it's as if your face against the sky
creates a single bolt of lightning

then time moves as a condition of winter

there's just the small person there
writing letters beside the old, blue horizon

with diminishment occurring earlier
coming from another person

then sun spilling over
makes it impossible to see them

the vagaries of weather resemble
pressures that cause panic and weeping
then "progress" makes a year delicious

there's just the hungry and thirsty person
speaking to the child   shaking so often in sunlight

Black Boxers : A Brief History

JACK JOHNSON (1878–1946)

Born to two former slaves,

Johnson triggered race riots after defeating the "Great White Hope" James Jeffries to maintain his title as first black heavyweight champion of the world.

For that fight, he won 1.6 million dollars, adjusted for inflation.

Convicted under the Mann Act aka the White Slave Traffic Act in 1912 for marrying Lucille Clifton, a white woman,

He fled the country until he ran out of money in 1920 after which he returned and served time in a federal penitentiary.

Johnson died in a car accident at age 68 after speeding away from a North Carolina diner that refused to serve him.

Sam Langford aka the Boston Tar Baby (1883–1956)

A renowned heavyweight who never held the world championship title.

Jack Johnson, the titleholder, refused to fight him.

He was afraid to lose to Langford and forgo the extra money he made by fighting white boxers on the other side of the color line.

When asked, Johnson said: "I'm the first black champion and I'll be the last."

Langford went blind and broke in Harlem, but after a *New York Herald Tribune* article raised money for his care, he spent his remaining days in a nursing home in Massachusetts.

Asked about his life shortly before his death, he remarked:

"Don't nobody need to feel sorry for old Sam.

I fought maybe 600 fights and every one was a pleasure."

Reggie Gross (1962—)

Raised by a single mother after his father was stabbed to death in a West Baltimore street fight when he was three days old.

Learned to fight at 13 after spending time in a juvenile detention facility for purse snatching.

After a brief light heavyweight career which culminated in a two-and-a-half minute Madison Square Garden loss to Mike Tyson in 1986,

Gross is now serving a life sentence for allegedly executing two drug dealers near a housing project in Baltimore that no longer exists.

Asked about his sentence, the prosecutor responded:

"If it all shakes out, he'll die in prison."

CLIFFORD ETIENNE AKA THE BLACK RHINO (1970—)

Learned to fight while serving a forty-year prison sentence for attempted armed robbery and became a professional boxer upon his parole in 1998.

Etienne had a 28-4-2 record, but is best known for losing in 48 seconds to Mike Tyson in 2003 at the Pyramid in Memphis, Tennessee.

After his career declined, he was incarcerated again in 2006 for robbing a check cashing business, carjacking and kidnapping a family, and attempting to shoot two police officers in Baton Rouge, Louisiana.

In 2013, his sentence was reduced from 160 years to 105 due to a procedural error.

Najai Turpin (1981–2005)

Turpin was a contestant on an NBC reality show, *The Contender*, which followed amateur boxers competing against one another to win a million dollars.

He grew up in a North Philadelphia housing project where he lost his mother at 18, after which, relatives say, he retreated emotionally.

After her death, he supported his younger siblings by working as a line cook before moving briefly to Los Angeles to take part in the show.

At 23, soon after *The Contender* ended, Turpin shot himself in the head while sitting with the mother of his daughter in a car outside the gym in West Philadelphia where he trained.

In a press conference shortly after his death, *Contender* producer Mark Burnett emphasized:

"These were not fish out of water, people placed in an unusually stressful situation.

This is a bunch of...highly trained young men doing what they normally do...

Fight each other with the goal to feed their families and try to achieve greatness."

I Just Want Us to Be On

Small lies change the brain's architecture making way for lyric verse
For people prepared to deny the need for the best we could do.

I become angry, move the anger into obscure deposits
And express its excess as the opposite of generosity.
I break into points and walk.

It makes sense to forget everything in advance.

Work, work, blue fear, hot reactive materials.
In the beyond-black of smoke, the brain's ball lightning.

If in a situation of regret, you let your anger become the law's
    terrible machine.
If in a situation of conflict, you work out.

When I tell you I'm not angry, you don't believe me. You're angry.
    You tell me you love me.
But we live in anger like the law. How do you love me if you don't
    believe me?

If in a situation of conflict, I let my anger become the law.
If I regret, I work.

I'm always sorry for what I fail to consider. But the audience has a way with words.
No more returning to the text to untuck living from casuistic dreams.

On the first night, I spoke up, then sound for a whole year.
Perceptual weaponry beyond the off-white horizon.

You try hard to increase your emotional storage.
How do people tell each other apart?

A coat of boiled wool, red and in motion.
A car accident. Then, they sew my head to your shoulders.

Every day from now beside ourselves,
the empty formalism of our early lessons.

One is an unbelievable number

His mother, like mine, was young when she had him though unlike me he was the oldest of two and had a sister. She and his father fought a lot, I gathered, it was occasionally physical. They had little money. She drank. His father was in medical school, owned a nursery with his brother, played a bass guitar, and drove an old Porsche, which formed the first fetishes of his child mind and called to him constantly thereafter. His father smoked marijuana and had a relationship with another man, an entomology professor at the university. I understand that it was sexual only through implication from third parties. He has never indicated it himself. We used to take that old man to the grocery. At every point, my understanding of the relation between things erases itself before stepping forward. When he was still young, his father and his uncle disappeared. Plane crashes in films now fill him with anxiety. *Cast Away*, for example. Was he truly anxious, I would wonder, or performing again to this particular audience. The last time they spoke he yelled at his father on the phone, for being absent maybe. His mother smoked and drank and was described to me as "not maternal." She remarried a chemist. They also fought. He has accessed such little distance. I don't ask questions that might illuminate and clarify these relationships, but what else is there to know. He fought with his stepfather and got in fights with black teenagers in a neighborhood where white people were few in number. He described the light imprint of his fist on black skin with nervous elation. Performing. It's a scene I never liked to imagine. He smoked marijuana and painted. Years later, I understood that his father appeared in dreams and offered something like resolution.

I hate the moment things begin to feel only intellectual. I lose exactly what it is that's being tracked. Nightmares become suddenly unimportant, which also disturbs. The last time he saw his mother, his stepfather had already died. We were at P.F. Chang's in Rookwood. My family, after all. The feeling of being followed. The memory of having thought about it as it happened. She was still young, but I felt even then there was nothing left. That horrible distance between gaze and presence. She could not follow conversation. Haunting, literally frequency. When she had a stroke, she called him. When he heard this poem, he was furious. But I know what I think about this record of white psychic death. It's a lesson I live with. It was late when she called him. He had been sleeping. He was upset.

they didn't know what they were smiling at / there was no image in the frame

surely it's no
accident   I'm drawn
to a figure in the road

a yellow raincoat
it's manufactured
centers all vision

says don't kill me
in the rain   I trust you
this means something

to us   this figure makes me
up then   a problem
left untended

I push the image forward
with cars   more rain   rowhouses
electric reds blues

associate it with work

there it was

and not knowing itself

I imagine

a person

the black sign

themselves   inside

a raincoat   I watch them

as they move

through falling water

as the narrative spills

as it fails

to show myself

the one object of my desire

inside the coat

it's yellow then

I cannot see a face

the face is so under

and I was paranoid

thinking how it would

be me in that

situation   against the cars

in yellow   black

produced by the situation

they anticipate

my mother of color loves me so much

      your voice was inside my body
then your image came apart inside my hands –
      in the lights , I'm dazzled , easily , in eye contact's bright wake where doors revolve , push air around in long pockets . at which point he asks " is that for here ?
      you said to go ? desire in daytime makes resonance in the photoelectric chamber , but I'm busy watching black content , occupied in small critique .
      I can't raise my voice , *maman* , I'll lose your face , *maman* , on camera , I'm worried I'll forget your blessing . my desolate acid jazz is back
      but this is *love when I'm around you* . (does pain always make for good art ? *dunno...ask him*) . I think you're just too good for me .
      when I see you from a distance I think no one's right , ever, just more or less in touch with the spirit's red unfolding . no one's *all* right
      not you or me . we're going to take this photo , aren't we ? I love to see how much we look alike

you scrutinize its face . meanwhile , it models yours .

eye music is an inside joke on the surface of manners
so , I thought , even here , the performer and composer
seem one and unhappy in the midst of this ecstatic plenitude ,

in a day dimmed by the distant patter of heads falling . *je vous suppli ,*
ma doulce damoyselle ; don't let iconography *get in the way*
of what I'm feeling . attachment is melismatic as it bobs

around a familiar center , as aporias in self-perception are filled
or , what , franchised to new owners ? in company , in crisis
with this , your riotous malfeasance . you actually have no idea

what love is – you wouldn't blow my phone with cruelty .
then , I see the parent in cold yellow light ,
action painted , yowling , shoulders bulged in oleaginous moaning .

think : wow , my consciousness is so so *centered*
      in the rally , on the steps ,

I live through love's gestalt : tall , violent , treacly ,
relentlessly polyphonic — still , I don't like
when you describe language as "rich ."

I do my best to complain

beautiful , good , wise

the raised voice is a high-pressure jet to the heart's black knocking —
what you want for me to confirm in you is impossible
young man sweet boy . that heart is all words , red notes ,

so you don't love when the room requires your laughter to function
glitches shake the blood machine , small beeping from radical cells
father , *I love you so well*

I have no other purpose . I write this poem from the bones of another
because I'd buried you there , in my shirts , speech , my attention
to suffering , in the razed earth

I make occur from inside my limbic motor . black is this bounty
that blooms even in the bright lights of the ER — a sign
under which I've grown so fast and angular

for example , I'm getting closer to saying : this is all you .
then I think that's not true or even useful .
spiritual suicide happens so fast . but

that's something I can't do . I'm in that night you had the knife
in the car .we were speeding so fast to Avondale ,
toward my mother and some man ,

beating through the black night . it was quiet . no birds sang .
no one moved . but she made it through — I did too .
maybe you didn't have it in you . maybe

I'm finally free to go ?

ECSTATICS

PRIVATE LOVE

REMEDIAL OUTRAGE

AND SO I WAS
UN ABLE

TO BE PROUD

SUCH SERIOUS TEARS

FROM MEN THIS WEEK

AND SO

YOU SAY

YOU SUFFER

BLACK
LOVE

YOU

TROPICAL
DELUSIONS

LOVE YOU

GOT TO BE

NECESSARY
EXTRAORDINARY

WASTE
MAN
    you
  POORNESS
    you
CLASS
POLITIC

BECAUSE WE ARE NOT

FREE / MY WORK

SO
I WAS

VERY BLUE

OPERATIC

A HAVEN

TRUE|OUT

SUPREME FORTRESS

PRIVATE NETWORK

THE PASSING

OF

A GREAT
INTUITION

WASTE
MAN
    you
POORNESS
    you
CLASS
POLITIC

FATHER

AMEN

SCATHED

DISORDERED

I ALLOW

YOU TO

SUFFER
ALONE

YOU

WEAPONIZE

CON

STRAINT

GRAPES

I CRIED THEN I WAS UNABLE TO GO FORWARD

if I'm walking in an urban situation I'm usually walking with someone
we on our own huh even if I make it early

if I'm in line any line   then , a disentangled grid
       equals a local battle

at the supreme north face drop for example
       inside a shirt or sneaker, time circulates

you know they locked in the first 25 people in the first gate ?
       and everybody else in the second gate
       and beyond got a number...

you know security is out here trying new procedures every week

in an urban situation , I'm usually walking with someone and shake
       I need a bite of chicken and we make a careful decision
       about a hat or costly tonal shift

we don't usually get that right
       we're not healthy so the situation dips to slow possession

can you tell us about the numbering system how it's working
    that's not wrought that's good
        that can be hard to think through ?

I'm usually walking or waiting with someone
    increasingly conscious of the barrier

an example of no flowers or shrapnel
    we're insulting the line from beside it

it's just people that wait in line from time then from there
    they give me my stuff then they eat
        soon we all eat ? just thinking that doesn't make sense

I was going forward after all I was planning
    to buy an expensive shirt not co-sign the situation of the street

I did that and I didn't   then I was walking suddenly

    with someone very different

PUBLIC STRAIN

       The most ecstatic anxiety
           Unchecked burst of rhododendron
Make my mind
        Available
             Conspicuous twitch of legal order
Anxious order of ecstasy
      Ecstatic burst of the law
           Makes my mind
     Percentage of melanin
            Rhododendrons blooming
    In a crowd
Availability of law
      Unchecked parentage
If
     Ecstasy twitches
            (Field blooming)
    What is my mind's
        Floral percentage
When
     Ecstasy is available
       Love bursts
         Law blooms

Been lynched enough
Slaved enough
Cried enough
Died enough [!]

Julia Fields

my head on the line's surface

on a train next to people

touching

THE POLITICS of INTIMATE SPACES (robust predictions in infinite horizons

It will be awkward so don't
I agree no in certain cases

You don't hear me when I talk
It might be mirrors, hate watching

That one gets so angry
Pushing people from the ring

So ordinary   I high five
the black hand of the future

I'm nervous you are
beside me clustering

Then people being
far off in authority

It might be loud I'm shy
I tried to turn into myself

I obviously don't know
the situation   it's so unmanageable
                              TRUE
                    ]   LOVE™

Keep it together
It will be awkward (! so don't

People believe they are   [CAPTIONED ?
In a manner of speaking (how could ? they're outlined

And they're killed by men with rifles
And they're fifteen and black and killed by rifles

                    [NOT RAW MATERIAL
And they're so awkward to hold

They accumulate heat, slow, sudden
Involuntarily, you lose one in the snow

Then someone *takes* vacations
Then apology works exceptionally on time

I feel like dying so often and shame
      [people starving , so angry

beside each other somehow

with no confidence arising

It just hurts to see you feeding

the situation   it's so awkward

                        ]   YOU WERE POULTRY

You think someone is all ready and declining

Between us this green and red and weight

I could spend my life in that laughter

in that terrible sleep

going into nights with guns in them

weeping in very narrow halls

YOU WERE POULTRY

(black river electrical burns

listen, I'm the earth that all these people died in
some grandparents, some germans, some lounge singers
and veterans   it's a human door

so when I *erupt* in *music*:
        chandeliers *collapse* and glass out
        the sun *soaring* past the collapsing sheet
    etc.   I've lolled myself to sleep

people have *energy*   they shock and hold you
inside a night with moonshine, debris streaking

inside a day with river, maraschino sun, overdose of sun,
and the president on the beach
                I get off the floor

then my voice projects from the dark side of its container
I wake from dreamless sleep to the soft anger of buses

this nightmare people press together

& if you're sad there's no being there anyway

                                                                ]   FAKE LOVE

so asymptotic

feral I love

people listen they make me nauseous

ACCIDENT FORGIVENESS

in trying to kill one kind of creature

we seem to struggle with precision

everything makes a sudden problem

the problem of poison, bycatch and net

that dying in the social

so when I miss you in a crowd

you call political

when your speech is clearly described

I miss you

I'm moving

I decided to *be* finally in a situation

forming bluebirds, love billowing

from the community & the imaginative

structures of the mind

this traumatic reaction

sometimes all I had was that

thinking of people

atop each other

mouths opening in air

even when I wanted most

to black someone out

I shaved with this feeling

I couldn't do it to people

shun, hurt, go on

so I hated Richard Serra

feeling small before

steel walls with money

in them, security

lurking   was there blood on me

I wondered ? was I just

another creature singing

CLUSTERING NOT ONLY DELUSIONS

real exhaustion
in the city, only people

SUPREME OPERAS

so I'm living strongly in the present , un-narcotized

and people join , they're not incorporated

    in love with my face in a storefront
      I'm neon blue water

sex, SZA, filming police on the street corner
    two people work all day then do a lot together

I find my body easy to accept, not simple   ,
   not all inside utterance which spreads itself
      flush against the edge of suffering (...

   I'm in love with the storefront, red
    manmade blackness

I'M a REAL FANTASY

  which is love to be there

I'm not smiling and the whole system of feeling must be sorry
    must be violent ? being in action

I pass by the Freedom Tower
    and watch the permanent day,
        LEDs shining frankly , light that doesn't love me

    I feel calm and that sense of swimming through foot traffic
        My foot falls cuz my attention is divided

& I'm in love with the water, with the artificially-colored
    I'm re-sensualizing the mirror
        of my natural environment

        so when I look into glass ,
            my face will helplessly occur

and I go to the shopping district
    where there's a strong wind moving

it blows the bags from me
    it creates a strong electric feeling
        I feel the wind from money circulating

    and I have no money so my face against
        glass is like a single bolt of lightning

UNEXPLAINABLY JUICY

I am sick *right now* an unelaborated box , so sick I forgot
    mixed race sociality
        fashionable pain sprouts   and clusters , ...

FRUITS form it's all good
FRUIT in my lungs it's a blessing

so people want permission to say the soul is at issue ...
    I'm so concerned I'm sick
        apple , banana

One thing is so close to another it becomes difficult
    to respond to that , open to a number of abuses
        re-presenting color

I am sick don't believe the hype
    (in New York , I muscle up , green light swirls ...

It's like everything is cursed !

Margaritas at the front door

Psychedelic fruits camouflage the front door

Oh my god we can't sit down, let people get run over
      by shame and prisons

Everything looks like a readymade, like a very serious rose at first

then FRUIT   fruit follows   red with seeds in it

the red riding hood of Rei Kawakubo

oh lord isn't that a further principle ? polyurethane resin and I'm on my way
    to fight the law for what they did to leisure

        no one should be happy while the water is poisoned
            and the South suffers
                while the police grow in capability

        no one should be *that* basis for the state of red

but don't I like to consume ? and produce with supreme pressure
    for the folks back home

        I wear my clothes unfitted cuz I'm out of time
        I wear the riding hood
            while my joy falls asleep

the future is manic nylon in our dreams the future is gunmetal
    the mental metropole
        in the forest with my neon fears   easy

        I listen to arpeggiated hi-hats in the hood I bought
with my future money ,
            I make a case against pain management

       and I fall in love with the feeling , twisted up
         and furious with luxury

then someone says *execute them* , the offense is grave or sufficient
    someone says jail , electric chair
      I go get my face from the floor

      and we say rest in peace to them
          for now , the wolves are still on top

but I've got my beauuuuutiful armor
    it's all lit up by fire

I WANT TO DIE IN DESIGNER

Jeans for the nude of my legs to rest on   you want

to know what I wear at home   A shirt

of pure cotton and I feel my life arrive

I meet myself in the mirror   I wear silk

to the station and walk through a checkpoint

of municipal law   I move toward Wall Street past

the federal courthouse

A wool sweater in midnight blue

a bed for my cotton shirt

cotton for the nude

of my chest   I am caught

in my condition   I am dwarfed

by the courthouse as I walk downtown

to meet you   I show no teeth

past the municipal checkpoints

Hair for the nude of my head

a hood I'm on my way to see you

so I pass the guns and checkpoints

wearing blue and black   branded shoes

and materials   Bone for the nude of my brain

We've barely met   I go through the eyes of the city

to reach you and spend some time

I'm covered in fabric I ask what it does

My body has an unknown name

and the right shirt can make me

throw it in the tall grass

I made a plan to see you

and I thought of who might see me

in the middle of my life

In the checkpoint I was all arms

all face   A quiet commercial played

in my heart   then

I felt the most ecstatic panic

SUFFERING PRIVATE LOVE

and living every day in the city

an OUTRAGE

> then I tried to articulate a relationship
> to *life* , its suddenly appearing

hey !

True Love I want
      Love looking for
           Love / True Love

not traffic
not shriveled grapes in perforated plastic
not this obvious purpling

I had to weep so openly
that my face withdrew from representation

and I'm on the curb sitting –
it's night, my nose is running,
my voice is wet with music

and I'm feeling very sorry
for the pain I pass on
(even when it shakes the sky
makes diamonds fall so beautifully
                      [truly

I want love all thirsty and spoken up
but there's no sound, no sun

just this dream of love,
while I sit and wait for what ?   a public service ,

the golden surface
of another person ?

GOD CAN YOU PLEASE HURRY AND FIND I WASN'T SURE THAT WE COULD BE

Can we say we , me more than all the others ?

Can we subject style to such rigorous accounting
    beach the vessel to save it ?

        asking such questions I think
    might be the plenum of the just , the right , the only rights
        (*MY ROLE MODEL FUCKED MY LIFE UP*
          increasingly wary of the males

    my money , moral projects , my manner
draped and derided by sitcoms , phantasms
        (spending everything on time

        So I was full
    of anger , grief , couldn't put tongue
        or wound in a public picture
            put pressure on the Word !

I'm in a store, state, or database
    they give me an eye , time's very hot moment

    Can we call that a hurry ?
        all night dreaming of a body

All night dreaming of my mother
    she's in the car , I'm in the CVS
    for her , then the manager

    thinks I've stolen

and I have   !   it's true love

    Sometimes we believe we're happy by loving

we reach out to each other in goodness
we work together to correct our misunderstandings

    but people don't always listen like that

they tell you war is natural and never-ending

I found it hard all my life

I hated it so much

IN POPEYES

*(the chamber won't produce resonant
volume , then love of the other moves
them to silence*

Characters

Rough Sleeper , they are *draped* in bright , weathered fabrics & don't find meaning , except by chance

Liz , the Resister in blue and troubled , is an investigator for the public defender's office , early 30s , falls in love easily , attracted to the rhizomatic figure

@PriyaTwoTimes , mournable without melancholy , a sister of two , owner /cashier

Shame doesn't believe in himself , falls asleep in the sleeper's ego

Tense Past is present

Setting

The Popeyes on 321 W. 125th St. in Harlem in the year of our lord , 2018 . It's February !

(throughout, the SCREEN plays text and epigraphs)

Scene

Rough Sleeper has been in this Popeyes for years . in fear , and tears about it . They see all . They interpolate Philoctetes.

Tense Past :
> I must care for myself ...
> Offend me . Tell me outrageous truths .
> There's no one here but us so you die
> & there's no black for you – the risk is that –
> there's no black because it doesn't exist .

Liz :
> I'm here for comfort . I'm here for footage
> from closed circuit cameras (nourishment
> in the limbic motor because the world ends
> with no prison in it .) There's only the hungry
> and thirsty child shaking at the Popeyes
> with people in it . A robbery occurred
> and my client needs a witness .

Rough Sleeper wails with their body .

The SCREEN reads: (Love streams from inside the room where chicken cooks .

Rough Sleeper :
> Closer . Closer . Friendship looks like this .

Their drapery moves as a harsh wind blows through . Liz
approaches (in) peace .

Rough Sleeper :
>I've been cast away ,
>so utterly alone where no one even walks by (Philoctetes) .
>Theft – its image descends in low resolve
>& I see men walk in , weak beside the spirit's
>red unfolding .
>we're red at the center of the ego!political
>so everything happens here . People move
>north , they paint the social channel blue .

Liz :
>You speak as if wounded , this drapery
>perpendicular to your low affect . You say " Haiti
>as if it doesn't happen *now* .

Rough Sleeper :
>I say it can't be now cuz nothing is .

Liz :
>(icily

Rough Sleeper :

    (praising Heaven

@PriyaTwoTimes :

    (as if RS is there but isn't happening) Can I help you ?

Liz :

    I have to see the footage , it's what I'm paid so little for .
    I called you to talk – your voice like
    two doves unspooling the thread of dawn .

@PriyaTwoTimes :

    And yours like a powdered jelly donut .
        Come closer . Friendship . I don't want to lose
    you in the corners of this room .

Liz :

    Do you have what we discussed ?

@PriyaTwoTimes :

    I have nothing .

Liz :

> Beautiful , but you'll slip away like that .

@PriyaTwoTimes :

> Don't be disappointed . We've met before .

Liz :

> I don't feel knowledge between us – there's a person here breaking in the far chair . You say you've known me yet you act as if they don't exist . Your politics confuse me What kind of place is this ?

@PriyaTwoTimes :

> Somewhere satisfied by the supply chain .
> > Chickens come in smaller parts , then
> > we quickly fill the register !
> > Don't @ me – ask the body in the seat .
> > You want crime & it can't occur without them .

Rough Sleeper is in agony .

Shame shrouds them in bad conscience , which is , at last , an ethical error .

Liz moves toward Rough and the light , that bright weight , oscillates in volume .

Liz :

    Will you speak ?

Rough Sleeper :

    (mortally

Liz :

    I see you suffer & I pity you .
    I can't fathom why you're here .

Rough Sleeper :

    In all I saw before me nothing but pain ;
    but of that a great abundance (P) . In the corner
    of the franchise where chicken is battered
    burned & spiced , where snow lines
    the street outside with luminous sheets .
    I can't sleep – I'm in a martial situation ,
    & competition comes from chains and start-ups .
    Marcus Garvey raps the door at night .
    I'm a black phantom . I can't die .

> I'm afraid Heaven is a stage for Al Jolson
> so my session state can't adjust .

Tense Past :

> They're here because you are –
> when you leave they disappear .

Rough Sleeper :

> (rougher) I can't die and enter light because there isn't any
> . I'm draped in the corner where crimes are recorded .
> I'm poisoned – my brain tastes my blood for it .

Liz :

> I can't help you , but I'd like to .
> I have to know what you've seen ,
> how you were feeling when you saw it .
> I want to see it too . I'll help you .

Rough Sleeper :

> I was blue in the social channel .
> . . I thought people don't come here
> to walk . They don't walk at all .
> They eat salt off the tables .

So a disruption in the social space
makes eyes fall with shame .
(from the heart)
The problem is you need crime as a concept
for this discourse to occur . You're not bad ,
but the dramatic situation supposes far too much .

L<small>IZ</small> :

    (depressed

L<small>IZ</small> :

    @PriyaTwoTimes ?

        !

@P<small>RIYA</small> :

    I am the vendor

    I am the vendor

    I am the vendor

        I believe in collaborative effort

            so long as it makes sense (Mach Hommy) .

S<small>HAME</small> begins to sweep the floors , severe but fashion .

Liz :

    I'm in a Freudian storm . My anger has turned
against me & my depression is severe .
My sense is that there's no talking . Not here ,
where shame darkens the tabletops
& joy has gone missing .
        My client is in cuffs –
she must be set free .
        (to Rough Sleeper)
You said you see but what you say
deflates me . The dramatic situation is one
& we are in it . There's everything else ,
but not for us & you don't want that
anyway .

Tense Past :

    (is a human being & they love their black mother .
You speak to the victim in pain , that ball
of fabric immolating in the eatery .

Liz :

    (severely

Rough Sleeper :

>From me , all has been taken & I live
as an object of scrutiny , a social problem .
Guns , homes , wallets with bills and cards .
I sit inside the chicken franchise
as True Love's VIP (Burial) .

Liz :

> & the police ?

Rough Sleeper :

> In a batch , they come for me .

Liz :

> (beseechingly

Rough Sleeper :

> You want cameras – they aren't possible .
> The image comes apart in your hands
> & lives its half-life inside me .

Liz :

> But they'll lock my client up ,
> far from those who know them !

Rough Sleeper :

> There's only Popeyes . Light , dark ,
> the carceral turn – chicken , gravy ,
> Cajun spices . There's only the hungry
> & thirsty person shaking so often
> in sunlight .

(Lights strobe briefly , then one minute of horrible silence , soft weeping brings us out)

Liz :

> (extravagantly
> (tears the drapery from Rough Sleeper , it overtakes the stage , is strewn about
>
> (committing spiritual suicide
> (Shame , Tense Past are lined up in the background

Liz :

>(as if of a police officer
>
>>Do you really think like that ?
>
>We're not *trapped* in the chamber ,
>singing quiet beside the deep fryers –
>What happens here touches the world
>where weavers sing beside the loom
>where synthetic color blooms
>even warmly in the night time .
>In other words , your quarantine exists
>but only in a social sense – it's not
>an argument for selfhood .

Rough Sleeper is divinely stressed .

Liz :

>Compromised , leaking in my old
>subject position – I promise I could
>love you soon , so much .

(Shame , Tense Past flagellate them softly , with silks , this noise is broadly heard

(after some time , Rough Sleeper has the last word

Rough Sleeper :

    (wrongheaded

        Repetition with a difference ,
ten to twelve AM every day except
for Christmas & Easter . I think
that chicken isn't infinite , but I woke
up here , my head was wet with fine spray (P)
& the chamber refused my cries .
        Holiness might not die either . but
there they are , with their theories
of criminal justice . There's just the child –
or is it just the chicken ? me & Liz – or just
the politicians ? Through the glass doors ,
people come and eat . Then they leave ,
& shoot one another in the head with roses .

*pleasure is stubborn /
in retrospect*

first there's love...then there's synchronized time
then there's troops barely secretly in Yemen ,
Niger , the pre-turnstile zone of the subway .
that's happening also . there are people out
and the sense that love can't *be* from them ,
can't be seen assuming
any kind of grace . *when you broke , you just feel*
abandoned , acrylic reds , yellows . I love you
cuz you're on the other side of the room ,
cuz steam comes off you in the twilight gone green
with night vision . I fall asleep by three , wake up
by nine , cuz the cars go by so harshly . then I think :
love is coming from me, love is *streaming*
from me . it's there, but there's no time .

ACKNOWLEDGMENTS

Some of the poems in this book borrow and reconfigure shards of language, lovingly and not so, from Kodwo Eshun's *More Brilliant Than the Sun: Adventures in Sonic Fiction* (London: Quartet Books, 1999), Burial's *Untrue* (Hyperdub, 2007), Future's "Damage" (*HNDRXX*, 2017), Julia Fields's "high on the hog" (1969), Jane Goodall, Charles Bernstein, Amiri Baraka, Isaiah Rashad's "Nelly" (2015), Adrienne Rich's "Waking in the Dark" (1972), Dean Blunt, Don Q, Beverly Dahlen's *A Reading 8-10* (Tucson, AZ: CHAX, 1992), Young Thug, Baude Cordier's "Belle, Bonne, Sage," Sonny Rollins, and W.E.B. Du Bois. Lyn Hejinian's *The Cell* (Los Angeles, CA: Sun & Moon Press, 1992) is the source of *"pleasure is stubborn / in retrospect,"* and Edmond Jabès's *The Book of Dialogue* (Middletown, CT: Wesleyan University Press, 1987) is the source of "you scrutinize its face." *In Popeyes* interpolates *Philoctetes* by Sophocles (trans. Richmond Lattimore). "to heaven , on a mule" is an ekphrastic critique of two films: Ken Jacobs's *Star-Spangled to Death* (2004) and the Al Jolson musical, *Wonder Bar* (1934). Wintertime's song of the same name is the source of "I Want to Die in Designer."

Thanks to Projective Industries for publishing poems from "GRAPES" as a chapbook of the same name in 2018 and to *The Recluse*, *Hyperallergic*, *Black Warrior Review*, *Sonora Review*, *Territory*, and *Tagvverk* for publishing earlier versions of some of these poems. Thanks to Blue Mountain Center and the Vermont Studio Center for the support. Thanks especially to Rachel Valinsky, Corinne Butta, Simran Ankolkar, Julia Andréone and Ghazaal Vojdani, and everyone at Wendy's Subway for bringing this book into the world with care, patience, and insight. Love and gratitude to all the friends, teachers, poets, and artists who shaped these poems in so many ways: An Duplan, Cindy Gao, Pierre Gergis, Christopher Harris, Kamden Hilliard, Livia Huang, Kirsten Ihns, Ethan Plaue, Saretta Morgan, Andrew J. Smyth, Kristen Steenbeeke, Simone White, Elizabeth Willis, and so many more. Love and thanks to my family. Rest in peace to my teacher Linda Bolton who taught me some strength and my grandma Gloria Nelson Turnbow who taught me some love while this book was being written.

What was I thinking ? I wrote : I don't believe in pulling events apart from one another

I was close to it , then I understood how exposure to death is a structural guarantee . So re: anxiety — I was looking hard at how to make some sense with suffering , to elaborate some consciousness through drones , writing to drones , drifting off , listening to rap music just words and code tumbling , pugilistic relationship to the material of sound . I felt a little ugly , then my inner light, I saw it beam and sweep around the room . I was getting my bag checked and swabbed every week , the police were heavy on every block , soldiers with rifles at the stations . I was watching Black people move from left to right across a hundred years of film and video , living chaotically , etc.

And my anger was so obvious, pressing its way up from my stomach . someone half-burned my apartment down , I almost wept , that dim and blown-out place . everything was ghosts and codes , ghosts and codes , this tense amniotic warbling

oh no , I don't like it , I thought and wrote , can't live in it . I wrote and the air popped off in these grim ecstatic colors

The sour world dripped , glowed